Agrarian Justice

By Thomas Paine

with a Foreword by

Nancy Altman

Dedication, Acknowledgment, and Foreword Text Copyright © 2015 Nancy Altman

All rights reserved.

ISBN: 1512210781
ISBN-13: 978-1512210781

DEDICATION

I dedicate the Foreword to three men—Robert M. Ball, Wilbur J. Cohen, and Robert J. Myers—who inspired me with their insight, depth of knowledge, compassion, determination, and dedication to Social Security. Highly principled, with enormous integrity, all three began working on Social Security in the 1930's and continued for as long as they were humanly able.

Bob Ball, dignified, personable, with a warm sense of humor and a razor-sharp mind, began his work with the Social Security Administration in the lowest level job at the lowest pay given an employee with a college degree. He rose from there to head the agency, becoming the longest-serving commissioner in the history of the program. Bob was the one who told me, in one of our many wide-ranging conversations, that Thomas Paine had proposed, in *Agrarian Justice*, old-age and disability benefits funded from an estate tax. A few months before Bob's death in 2008, he authored an op-ed in the *Washington Post* advocating that the federal estate tax be dedicated to Social Security and arguing, contrary to conventional thinking, that it was the height of responsibility to resist benefit cuts. It is no exaggeration that every single American, young and old, rich and poor, from every walk of life and from every ethnic background—all Americans—had a tireless advocate for the seven decades that Bob worked on Social Security. Though his name is not known to most Americans, he has perhaps done more to protect and expand their economic security than any other American, living or dead.

Wilbur Cohen, energetic, gregarious, and generous, began working on Social Security in 1934, the year before the program was enacted. He had numerous high level government positions, rising to become Secretary of

Health, Education, and Welfare (now Health and Human Services), as well as serving on the faculties of both the University of Michigan at Ann Arbor and the University of Texas at Austin. Along with Bob Ball, he was instrumental in the enactment of Medicare and Medicaid, as well as playing a role in every major piece of Social Security legislation. The late Senator Paul Douglas once quipped, "an expert on Social Security is a person who knows Wilbur Cohen's phone number." Wilbur died in 1987, in Seoul, South Korea, where he had flown to deliver a paper, "Aging and Welfare for the Aged," at a symposium. Like Bob, his contributions to our country are enormous.

Robert J. Myers, a shy, soft-spoken actuary, also began working on Social Security in 1934. He remains the longest serving Chief Actuary in the history of the program. Scrupulously honest, meticulous, and careful with his numbers, he was trusted by Democrats and Republicans alike. His integrity helped to establish the Office of the Actuary at the Social Security Administration as above repute, whose numbers were developed free of partisan pressure. The late Senator Daniel Patrick Moynihan (D-NY) dubbed Bob, "a national treasure." Like his colleagues Bob Ball and Wilbur Cohen, Bob Myers continued to work on Social Security in the United States and around the world until he no longer was able. He died in 2010. He, like Bob and Wilbur, exemplified the best in public service, working tirelessly for the benefit of his fellow Americans.

I continue to be inspired by the memory of all three men. I miss all three. To them, I dedicate my Foreword.

CONTENTS

Acknowledgments	vii
Foreword	1
Inscription to the French Edition by Thomas Paine	20
English Preface by Thomas Paine	23
Agrarian Justice	24

ACKNOWLEDGMENTS

I wish to thank my friend and colleague, Eric R. Kingson, with whom I founded Social Security Works. He and I have been partners every step of the way in building Social Security Works and the broad-based, diverse coalition it staffs. I wish to acknowledge, as well, Alex Lawson whose tireless energy and creativity have helped the idea of expanding Social Security take root. It was Alex's idea to republish Paine's *Agrarian Justice* with a foreword.

Readers should note that some material in the Foreword is drawn from Eric's and my co-authored work, *Social Security Works! Why Social Security Isn't Going Broke and How Expanding It Will Help Us All* (The New Press, 2015). Material is also drawn from Altman, "The Striking Superiority of Social Security in the Provision of Wage Insurance," 50 Harvard Law School Journal on Legislation 109 (2013), available at http://www.harvardjol.com/archive/volume-50-number-1/

THOMAS PAINE

FOREWORD

SOCIAL SECURITY, THOMAS PAINE, AND THE SPIRIT OF AMERICA

BY NANCY J. ALTMAN
FOUNDING CO-DIRECTOR
SOCIAL SECURITY WORKS

In a June 8, 1934 message to Congress, President Franklin D. Roosevelt announced his intention to propose Social Security. "I place the security of the men, women and children of the Nation first," he proclaimed. "If, as our Constitution tells us, our Federal Government was established among other things, 'to promote the general welfare,' it is our plain duty to provide for that security upon which welfare depends."

He assured Congress and the American people that Social Security would "not require the creation of new and strange values. It is rather the finding of the way once more to known, but to some degree forgotten, ideals and values."

Toward the end of his message he restated that important point:

> This seeking for a greater measure of welfare and happiness does not indicate a change in values. It is rather a return to values lost in the course of our economic development and expansion.[1]

Our Shared Ideals, Values and Heritage

A return to values, indeed. Thomas Paine was the brilliant writer whose 1776 essay, *Common Sense*, inspired his fellow colonists to turn their unrest into action and declare independence from Britain. Thomas Paine's visionary writings embody the spirit of our nation.

---

[1] President Roosevelt's *Message to Congress Reviewing the Broad Objectives and Accomplishments of the Administration, June 8, 1934,* available at http://www.ssa.gov/history/fdrstmts.html#message1

During the American Revolution, when General George Washington and his troops were forced to retreat to Valley Forge, it was Thomas Paine who wrote the stirring words that inspired those troops to fight on, despite the suffering and the odds. Paine's words were read as well by President Roosevelt in a fireside chat just a few short months after Pearl Harbor.

Like President Washington, who ordered that Paine's words be read aloud to his starving, freezing troops, President Roosevelt employed the words to encourage a worried nation embarking on a long and difficult war. On February 23, 1942, President Roosevelt told his fellow citizens:

> The task that we Americans now face will test us to the uttermost. Never before have we been called upon for such a prodigious effort. Never before have we had so little time in which to do so much.
>
> 'These are the times that try men's souls.' Tom Paine wrote those words on a drumhead, by the light of a campfire. That was when Washington's little army of ragged, rugged men was retreating across New Jersey, having tasted nothing but defeat.
>
> And General Washington ordered that these great words written by Tom Paine be read to the men of every regiment in the Continental Army, and this was the assurance given to the first American armed forces:
>> 'The summer soldier and the sunshine patriot will, in this crisis, shrink from the service of their country; but he that stands it now, deserves the love and thanks of man and woman. Tyranny, like hell, is not easily conquered; yet we have this consolation with us, that the harder the sacrifice, the more glorious the triumph.'
>
> So spoke Americans in the year 1776.
>
> So speak Americans today![2]

And Thomas Paine, the visionary American patriot and hero, wrote other timeless words that capture the spirit of America. In 1795 and 1796, he

---

[2] The entire text of the fireside chat is available at http://www.presidency.ucsb.edu/ws/?pid=16224

wrote *Agrarian Justice*, reprinted in the pages that follow.[3] In it, he calls for universal old age pensions as well as pensions for people with disabilities—ideas enacted a century and a half later in the form of our Social Security system.[4]

Far-sighted as Paine was, he saw even beyond today. He also proposed that young adults receive payments, when they reach the age of 21:

> When a young couple begin the world, the difference is exceedingly great whether they begin with nothing or with [a lump-sum cash payment] apiece. With this aid they could buy a cow, and implements to cultivate a few acres of land; and instead of becoming burdens upon society...would be put in the way of becoming useful and profitable citizens.

Thomas Paine understood the importance of preventing poverty before it occurs. While welfare helps people who are already poor, Social Security prevents workers and their families from falling into poverty in the first place.[5] So would Paine's proposed payments to young adults:

> It is the practice of what has unjustly obtained the name of civilization (and the practice merits not to be called either charity or policy) to make some provision for persons becoming poor and wretched only at the time they become so. Would it not, even as a matter of economy, be far better to adopt means to prevent their becoming poor? This can best be done by making every person

---

[3] Paine's opening words in his inscription to the French edition state, "THE plan contained in this work is not adapted for any particular country alone: the principle on which it is based is general." It was written when Paine was in France, during the French Revolution. (He describes the Reign of Terror as "execrable.") The focus in this Foreword is the U.S. Social Security system and the values and ideals espoused in Agrarian Justice that are embodied in the uniquely American institution. All direct quotes that are not cited are from the text of *Agrarian Justice*.

[4] Social Security is wage insurance, while Paine proposed demogrants—payments based simply on demographic status—but the essence and basic rationale are the same. In addition to benefits for workers who have achieved old age or who have serious and permanent disabilities, Social Security also provides benefits to the families of retired and disabled workers, as well as to the families of workers who have died.

[5] Social Security is designed to protect against significant financial losses and risks. Alleviating and preventing poverty is a byproduct of that goal. Not everyone who receives Social Security would be poor without it, but all would be poorer, and around half would have incomes too low to maintain basic subsistence.

when arrived at the age of twenty-one years an inheritor of something to begin with.

Imagine Thomas Paine's vision realized. Rather than so many of today's young people starting adulthood with mountains of student loan debt, every American would enter adulthood with a small lump sum to begin his or her career and family. Perhaps someday we will catch up to Paine's vision.

Indivisible, with Liberty and Justice for All

But we have caught up with regard to Social Security. As Thomas Paine advocated, Social Security is for everyone, rich and poor alike:

> It is proposed that the payments…be made to every person, rich or poor. It is best to make it so, to prevent invidious distinctions. It is also right it should be so….

It is a clever sound bite to assert that billionaires do not need Social Security and therefore should not get the benefits they have earned. But need has nothing to do with it. Paine's view that the rich should receive benefits is even more compelling in the context of today's Social Security system, whose benefits are part of the compensation packages of workers. Social Security benefits are earned through work and the payment of insurance contributions or premiums. No benefit is paid unless the worker has worked long enough and sufficient premiums have been paid. When that happens, the worker is insured, a status that must be met before any benefits can be paid to that worker and his or her family.[6]

For the wealthy who don't need Social Security, Paine had a solution, "Such persons as do not choose to receive it can throw it into the common fund." President George Washington refused to take a salary, receiving only living expenses. President John F. Kennedy chose also to turn down his salary as President, taking only $1 a year. No one is forced to take compensation. Anyone is free to not claim Social Security, make a gift to

---

[6] Workers who have contributed to Social Security for forty "quarters of coverage," up to a maximum of four quarters in any calendar year, are "fully" insured for benefits. In 2015, credit is given for a quarter of coverage for contributions made on at least $1,220 of earnings anytime in the calendar year. Because workers can become disabled or die at any time, workers may become insured for those benefits with fewer than forty quarters. For disability insurance benefits, there is an additional requirement that work have been recent.

the Social Security trust funds, or do both. Indeed, Social Security does receive gifts, carefully reported in its annual Trustees Reports.[7]

That is a generous, public-spirited act, as was Washington's and Kennedy's choice to forgo their presidential salaries. But everyone, rich and poor, should have the right to receive the compensation he or she has earned. That includes the compensation of Social Security.

The universality on which Social Security is based, a universality which Paine proposes, is captured in our nation's name, the *United* States, and in our pledge of allegiance which refers to an *indivisible* nation, not a land of the rich and everyone else. Social Security embodies the idea that we are one nation, sharing common risks, responsibilities, and rewards.

The program reflects other basic American values, as well. Our pledge of allegiance highlights our commitment to liberty and justice for all. A few, outside the mainstream, have argued over the years that Social Security restricts liberty, but the overwhelming majority of Americans understand that Social Security, which provides a guaranteed source of income that one cannot outlive, enhances freedom.

Before Social Security, most seniors, people with serious and permanent disabilities, and children who had lost parents had no choice other than to move in with relatives. If that was impossible, older people and people with disabilities invariably wound up in the poorhouse; children, even those still with a living parent, often were reluctantly placed in an orphanage. Today, Social Security provides some freedom of choice that comes with a guaranteed income.

Because Social Security is insurance that is universal and earned, it provides independence and dignity. And Americans understand that the program is just and fair in its design.

Means-Testing Social Security Would Destroy It

On April 14, 2015, New Jersey Governor, and Presidential hopeful, Chris Christie labeled Social Security an "entitlement" and proposed to take away the Social Security benefits of those with incomes over $200,000.[8]

---

[7] In 2012, for example, Social Security received about $1,000 in gifts.
[8] The text of the Christie speech, delivered in New Hampshire, is available at http://blogs.wsj.com/metropolis/2015/04/14/n-j-gov-chris-christies-speech-on-proposed-changes-to-social-security/

Governor Christie is only the most recent politician to call for means-testing Social Security. That change would radically alter and destroy our Social Security system as we know it. That might sound hyperbolic, but it is not.

Governor Christie and other opponents of Social Security seem to think Social Security is charity or, more pejoratively, a government handout. It is not. It is insurance that is earned and paid for. Opponents of Social Security willfully refuse to acknowledge that Social Security is an earned benefit, but the overwhelming majority of Americans understand it.

Social Security lifts more than 22 million people—including over one million children–out of poverty each year, and lessens the depth of poverty for many millions more. It is the nation's most effective anti-poverty program. But that is a byproduct of its goal, which is to provide universal insurance against the loss of wages.

Means-testing Social Security would radically transform it from what it now is. A means or affluence test would, in Thomas Paine's words, introduce invidious distinctions and would subtly but profoundly change Social Security so that it would no longer be insurance but instead would become welfare.[9]

Social Security Is Insurance, Not Welfare

The distinction between Social Security, whose goal is the maintenance of living standards when wages are gone, and welfare, whose goal is the assistance of those who are poor, is fundamental and sharp. Viewing Social Security simply as a government transfer program blurs this essential distinction. Too many policymakers today do not understand this crucial difference.

Social Security and the nation's welfare programs are intrinsically different, having developed from two separate and distinct historical roots. The antecedents to modern welfare can be traced to Biblical prescriptions,

---

[9] Those involved in the welfare rights movement of the late 1960's and early 1970's believed that poor Americans should be entitled to a guaranteed income as a matter of right under the Constitution. Unfortunately, the courts did not agree, nor has that ever been a dominant political sentiment. Whether considered a right or not, welfare, as this Foreword explains, is different from Social Security and other forms of social insurance.

such as the commandment that "thou shalt not wholly reap the corners of thy field, neither shall thou gather the gleanings of thy harvest. And thou shalt not glean thy vineyard...; thou shalt leave them for the poor..."[10]

In England, the practice of voluntary tithing to the Church to help the poor evolved into compulsory tithing, then into the English poor laws, and then to America's welfare laws, which were transplanted from England by the colonists. Those early welfare arrangements evolved into today's means-tested welfare programs.

In contrast, a second, equally rich, but fundamentally different practice dates at least as far back as the Middle Ages in England and Europe. Individuals who had a common trade or craft joined together to form mutual aid societies or guilds, which provided a variety of wage-replacement benefits to their members, in addition to regulating the craft. Similarly, in the mining districts of central Europe as far back as the sixteenth century, workers formed customary funds, which provided benefits for sickness and accidents.

Building on these models of pooled risk, Chancellor Otto von Bismarck was the first to provide nationwide compulsory, universal social insurance. The concept of government-sponsored insurance spread around the world, including to the United States, most notably in the form of Social Security.

A comparison of Social Security and the Supplemental Security Income program ("SSI") illuminates the stark differences between insurance and welfare. Both programs provide benefits to people who are old and to people with disabilities. But Social Security is insurance, where workers must work sufficiently long to be eligible for benefits. SSI is welfare, where recipients must be in need to receive benefits.

SSI, like virtually all welfare programs, pays a benefit that is designed to provide the recipient with just enough to get by, to subsist, as judged by those creating the program.[11] Benefit eligibility and amount depend on the potential recipient's income and assets. By definition, if the potential recipient is earning income above the subsistence level, he or she is not in need of the community's help. Even if the person is earning below the subsistence level, he or she is not in as great need as someone without earnings. Consequently, earnings result in reduced benefits up to the point

---

[10] *Leviticus* 19:9–10 (King James).
[11] The maximum federal benefit paid in 2015 to individuals with no income or assets is $733. Some states have chosen to supplement the federal benefit.

where those earnings are sufficiently large to eliminate the benefit altogether.[12] Similarly, if the person has savings or other nonwage income upon which to draw, he or she is not in need of the assistance of others. Nonwage income, like interest on savings, also reduces or eliminates SSI benefits. Individuals with savings of just $2,000 are ineligible for SSI.[13]

Under SSI's design, which is typical of virtually all welfare programs, work performed by SSI recipients is in effect not as well remunerated as it is when performed by non-SSI recipients.[14] Furthermore, thrift is penalized.[15] Moreover, in order to ensure that the income and assets limitations are not exceeded, SSI recipients are required to regularly report to the government numerous details of their lives. Recipients must report, for example, if they move, if others move in with them, or if household members move out. Every month, they must send all pay stubs to the government. All gifts, including such items as groceries bought by children, must be reported, as well.

Unlike SSI and other welfare programs, Social Security encourages work and savings. The higher one's earnings that are insured and the longer one works, the larger the benefit received. Savings are immaterial to the determination of Social Security benefits. Because Social Security's benefits are too low to allow most workers to maintain their standards of living in

---

[12] The first $65 of earnings in a month is disregarded. After that amount of earnings, every dollar earned reduces a recipient's SSI benefit by fifty cents.

[13] Nonwage income reduces a recipient's monthly SSI benefit dollar for dollar, after the first $20 of income, which is disregarded.

[14] To illustrate, take a minimum wage job, paying $7.25 an hour. Thanks to the earnings disregard, about the first 9 hours of work each month pay the full $7.25. After that, though, every hour of work increases total income by only $3.13, because the worker's SSI benefit is reduced by $3.13. That is the equivalent of a 50 percent tax on those earnings, because total income goes up by only half the wages earned. The reduction in SSI benefits as the result of work is not higher than 50 percent presumably to seek to ensure that there is some financial return for work. It is instructive to note that the top federal income tax rate is just 39.6 percent, and that is on an individual's income only in excess of $413,201!

[15] Interest on savings in a bank account results in no increased income overall, once the $20 disregard is exhausted, because the SSI benefit goes down dollar for dollar by the amount of that interest. Total income—the SSI benefit plus the interest on savings—is the same as if there were no savings. Most people, of course, want some savings in case of an emergency, but, in addition to the dollar-for-dollar reduction in benefits caused by the interest, savings of more than $2,000 ($3,000 for a married couple); disqualify an individual from receiving SSI altogether.

retirement, savings are encouraged. Moreover, Social Security beneficiaries are not required to file burdensome and intrusive reports about the details of their lives. They may receive groceries or other assistance from children without having to report that fact to the government or having it reduce their Social Security benefit by even a penny.

But perhaps the most fundamental difference between Social Security and welfare is this: To qualify for and continue to receive welfare, recipients must prove something negative about themselves (or at least, what many Americans consider negative)—that they do not have enough to get by on their own. In contrast, Social Security beneficiaries must prove something positive—that they have worked and contributed long enough to qualify for benefits.

A primary shortcoming of SSI and other means-tested welfare, where eligibility and benefits are based on need, was captured incisively and insightfully by Thomas Paine when he cautioned against "invidious distinctions." Welfare programs, modern and ancient, involve arrangements among financially unequal parties—those materially better off providing assistance to those less advantaged. A better approach, one that avoids those invidious distinctions decried by Paine, would be a minimum guaranteed income provided to all Americans, combined with a truly progressive income tax. Unfortunately, because a guaranteed minimum income has never been a popular concept in the United States, means-tested welfare is essential. In a nation as wealthy as ours and one that values compassion, those programs should provide adequate benefits, growing with the nation's increasing productivity and wealth, and people receiving those subsistence benefits should be treated with respect and dignity.

But what should not happen is the radical transformation of Social Security into welfare, as Governor Christie and other leading politicians have proposed, by eliminating the benefits of anyone who has earned them, but does not "need" them. To take an extreme example, imagine restricting Social Security to those with wealth of less than $10 million. Instead of simply showing, as you do now, that you have worked and contributed long enough to receive Social Security, you would instead have to prove to the government, through income tax returns, house valuations, and other evidence, that you are not too rich to receive Social Security.

That would turn the program on its head. Today, Social Security beneficiaries are deservedly proud of having earned their Social Security and rightfully claim that part of their compensation. That sense of pride in an earned benefit would disappear if Americans instead had to show that they weren't too successful to receive Social Security.

An American Solution to Our Shared Risks and Responsibilities: Social Security Funded by a Tax on Large Estates

While Thomas Paine wisely saw that a universal program would "prevent invidious distinctions," he also understood that those distinctions can evaporate in an instant. One's economic status can change drastically over time. Income and savings can disappear as the result of innumerable events including illness, the death of a spouse, or a bad economy. As Paine succinctly notes:

> I have no idea [if the benefits] would be accepted by many persons who had a [sizable] yearly income…But as we often see instances of rich people falling into sudden poverty, even at the age of sixty, they would always have the right of drawing all the arrears due to them.

This is as much a problem today as it was over 200 years ago. Take the case of Neil Friedman. Once a millionaire, he saw virtually all of his life's savings vanish on December 11, 2008, when Bernie Madoff's Ponzi scheme became public. Friedman had invested $4 million with Madoff. He never had an inkling that Madoff's investments were fraudulent until the day he learned that the money was gone. Now in his early eighties and widowed, he is fortunate to have Social Security to pay his bills.

As humans, we are all subject to common risks. Any of us today can get hit by a car or be stricken with cancer. On a happier note, all of us hope to grow to old age. Social Security is there to replace our wages if we suffer a serious, permanent disability, die leaving dependents, or live to very old age. One can outlive savings, but not Social Security.

Thomas Paine recognized our shared risks of disability and old age (which is a risk in the financial sense). In *Agrarian Justice*, he proposed a solution to deal with them. He also understood that we each have responsibilities. Out of that recognition, he proposed a thoroughly modern way to pay for his visionary plan. He proposed a tax on estates.

We the People Forming a More Perfect Union

Paine's proposal of an estate tax aligns perfectly with the values and ideals that motivated the founding of our nation. He was spurred to publish

Agrarian Justice—which he had already written but was holding for the right moment—by a sermon he found extremely objectionable. The title of the sermon says it all: "The Wisdom and Goodness of God, in having made both Rich and Poor."

Similar sentiments have been expressed throughout history by those who, as the quip goes, were born on third base and think they hit a triple. Those who have benefited the most in life often seem to justify their privileged positions as solely the result of their superior talent or even God's will. They wear their privilege with arrogance and a smug sense that this is the natural order of things, rather than accepting their wealth with humility, gratitude, and self-awareness of their good luck.

But Thomas Paine, patriot and clear thinker that he was, understood the truth. In response to the Bishop who preached that God in His goodness and wisdom created rich and poor, Paine responded:

> It is wrong to say God made *rich* and *poor;* He made only *male* and *female,* and He gave them the earth for their inheritance.
>
> Instead of preaching to encourage one part of mankind in insolence . . . it would be better that priests employed their time to render the general condition of man less miserable than it is. Practical religion consists in doing good: and the only way of serving God is that of endeavoring to make His creation happy. All preaching that has not this, for its object is nonsense and hypocrisy.

Thomas Paine and our other Founders understood that no one becomes rich completely on his or her own; no one is totally self-made. The accumulation of large estates is dependent, in part, on the nation's infrastructure. Governments build the public roads which assist getting goods to market, establish laws and courts that make contracts enforceable, fund police and fire services which protect property, and provide countless other goods and services benefiting rich and poor alike.

Indeed, the wealthy often benefit the most from what government provides. When government protects private property, for example, the rich have the most property to be protected. Thus, requiring the very wealthiest estates to contribute a portion of their great fortunes to the funding of common goods and services, while still retaining for heirs the large bulk of the assets accumulated, is the least that should be required of those who have benefited so greatly from the Commonwealth (i.e., common wealth).

President Barack Obama was widely mocked by conservatives during the 2012 election, when he inartfully and ambiguously uttered the words, "If you've got a business, you didn't build that." That sentence was taken out of context; he was talking about roads and bridges. Making the same point much more clearly and vividly, Thomas Paine wrote:

> Land…is the free gift of the Creator in common to the human race. Personal property is the *effect of society;* and it is as impossible for an individual to acquire personal property without the aid of society, as it is for him to make land originally.
>
> Separate an individual from society, and give him an island or a continent to possess, and he cannot acquire personal property. He cannot be rich.

Please pause here to absorb Thomas Paine's point. If a person were provided any island or continent in the world, but lived there in isolation from others, not only would he or she not become rich, that person would be fortunate to survive at all. If the individual did survive, he or she might have plentiful food. If clever and skilled enough, that person might have a nice home and clothes. But from where would the riches come? To whom would that person sell goods or services? There would be no commerce, nothing to buy or sell. Vast material accumulation would be impossible.

The Rich Owe a Debt to Society

Thomas Paine explained that those who are rich owe a debt to the rest of us:

> All accumulation…of personal property, beyond what a man's own hands produce, is derived to him by living in society; and he owes on every principle of justice, of gratitude, and of civilization, a part of that accumulation back again to society from whence the whole came.

As Paine, among the most eloquent in expressing America's founding ideals, so powerfully articulates, people who have benefited so greatly owe a debt to society. As a matter of justice, the rich owe a portion of their accumulated wealth back to society.

Paine then sharpened the point. He noted that, in many cases, the wealth was obtained in unjust ways so the obligation to pay back a part of those riches is even greater:

> This is putting the matter on a general principle, and perhaps it is best to do so; for if we examine the case minutely it will be found that the accumulation of personal property is, in many instances, the effect of paying too little for the labor that produced it; the consequence of which is that the working hand perishes in old age, and the employer abounds in affluence.

This latter point is all too apparent in today's America. America's workers are extremely productive. They work longer than workers in other industrialized countries. Yet in the last thirty years every penny of aggregate income growth created by all of that American productivity has gone to the top 10 percent. All of it. Indeed, most of it has gone to the top one percent!

Many elites are quick to charge that those who point out that stark fact and conclude that the wealthy are not paying their fair share toward the common good are engaged in so-called class warfare and the politics of envy. This allegation is not new. Thomas Paine answered the charge in *Agrarian Justice*. There he said:

> I care not how affluent some may be, provided that none be miserable in consequence of it. But it is impossible to enjoy affluence with the felicity it is capable of being enjoyed, while so much misery is mingled in the scene. The sight of the misery, and the unpleasant sensations it suggests, which, though they may be suffocated cannot be extinguished, are a greater drawback upon the felicity of affluence than the proposed [tax] upon property is worth. He that would not give the one to get rid of the other has no charity, even for himself.

Paine's comment that those who resist a reasonable estate tax have no charity, not even for themselves, displays a profound insight. Some who have accumulated great wealth seem never to feel that they have enough. Perhaps it is from an insatiable emotional need, coupled with a lack of compassion even for themselves, that some with wealth assume those not as financially fortunate are envious. But envy is not what drove Paine, nor indeed what drives today's sentiment toward the rich. Rather, the driving force is a sense of what is just and right. Articulating how many of us feel, Paine described his own attitude:

> Though I care as little about riches as any man, I am a friend to

riches because they are capable of good.

Requiring that the Rich Pay Their Fair Share

In what manner should the wealthy pay their debt to society? How best can the wealth, which, in Paine's words, is "capable of good," be employed for the common good? Over two hundred years ago, Thomas Paine explained why it is not enough for people of great wealth to give back only through personal charity. As important and admirable as private charity is, Paine explained the reason that government action is essential:

> There are, in every country, some magnificent charities established by individuals. It is, however, but little that any individual can do, when the whole extent of the misery to be relieved is considered. He may satisfy his conscience, but not his heart. He may give all that he has, and that all will relieve but little. It is only by organizing civilization upon such principles as to act like a system of pulleys, that the whole weight of misery can be removed.
>
> The plan here proposed will reach the whole. It will immediately relieve and take out of view three classes of wretchedness—the blind, the lame, and the aged poor; and it will furnish the rising generation with means to prevent their becoming poor…

And he made clear that the guiding principle should not be charity:

> But it is justice, and not charity, that is the principle of the plan. In all great cases it is necessary to have a principle more universally active than charity; and, with respect to justice, it ought not to be left to the choice of detached individuals whether they will do justice or not. Considering, then, the plan on the ground of justice, it ought to be…national and not individual.

What is the best way for the United States to require that those who have benefited the most from our common wealth pay the debt that they owe? A progressive income tax is one way, though high-priced lobbyists in today's world have done what they can to make the tax progressive in name only. The effective rate of taxation that the wealthy pay, as the multi-billionaire Warren Buffet has said, is often less than the rate paid by Americans of modest means.

Even more progressive is a tax on large estates, as Thomas Paine advocated around the time of the nation's founding, and was first enacted on a federal level in 1797.[16] Today's opponents of the federal estate tax have cleverly labeled it a death tax, but as Paine himself pointed out, there is no such thing.

When people die, their identities die with them. They cease to exist, at least in bodily form. They cannot sue or be sued. They cannot enter into contracts. They do not pay taxes. The instant they die, a new legal entity is born: the estate. It is a legal construct, as are, for example, corporations and trusts. When, during the 2012 election, Mitt Romney famously exclaimed, "Corporations are people too, my friend," it was humorous because corporations do not live and breathe, but corporations are arrangements to which the law gives an independent identity. Similarly, when a person dies, that person's property becomes the possession of a new entity with its own independent identity, the decedent's estate. Estates, like people, can sue and be sued. They can enter into contracts. And they can pay taxes. But they do not live and breathe and they do not die. Taxing an estate is taxing an artificial entity, not a dead person and not a dead person's heirs.

Thomas Paine understood this basic fact, even if today's opponents of the estate tax willfully refuse to acknowledge it. In arguing for a tax on estates, Paine commented:

> Various methods may be proposed for [funding the proposed program of benefits], but that which appears to be the best...is at the moment that property is passing by the death of one person to the possession of another. In this case, the bequeather gives nothing: the receiver pays nothing. The only matter to him is that the monopoly of natural inheritance, to which there never was a right, begins to cease in his person. A generous man would not wish it to continue, and a just man will rejoice to see it abolished.

The Estate Tax Embodies American Values and Ideals

It is no surprise that Thomas Paine, whose words so embody the spirit of the American Revolution, would understand how perfectly the idea of an estate tax fits within the ideals of our nation. The War for Independence sought to rid America of royalty, aristocracy, and entitled nobility. The Founders proclaimed that we are all created equal. Inherited wealth is at odds with the idea of a meritocracy, a nation where all are born with equal

---

[16] In 1797, Congress levied a tax on bequests larger than $50. The size of the tax increased with the size of the bequest.

opportunities to succeed.

Not that an estate tax would even come close to achieving a true meritocracy. Paine's proposal, just like today's federal estate tax, permits the bulk of wealth to "descend in a direct line to sons and daughters." Indeed, today's federal estate tax includes an unlimited marital deduction. That means that all property, even if worth billions and billions of dollars, can be left tax-free to a spouse. And $5.43 million ($10.86 million, per couple) can be left tax-free to children or other heirs. Today, 99.8 percent of all estates pay no estate tax whatsoever. Only a miniscule number—0.2 percent—of estates pay even a penny in federal estate taxes. Because of deductions and other offsets, those 0.2 percent of the nation's estates, on average, are able to retain five-sixths of the estate for heirs; only one-sixth is, on average, paid for the common good. But at least that small percentage, 16.6 percent, is paid back.

A Tax on Legacies to Pay a Legacy Debt

But why dedicate this tax to Social Security? The late Robert M. Ball is widely acknowledged to have been, at the time of his death in 2008, the foremost expert in the world on the U.S. Social Security system. To this day, he remains the longest-serving Commissioner of Social Security in the history of the program, having served under three presidents, two Democrats and one Republican. When he died, the *Washington Post* ran an obituary, entitled "Robert M. Ball: 'Spiritual Leader' of Social Security."

Agreeing with Thomas Paine, Bob Ball called for the dedication of the federal estate tax to Social Security.

> ...I propose to establish a new source of funding [in addition to the existing sources] by changing the estate tax into a dedicated Social Security tax....
>
> Present law gradually reduces the estate tax....President [George W.] Bush [who was president when these words were written] then wants to abolish the estate tax permanently....Instead, I would...earmark the proceeds for Social Security..., thereby converting the residual estate tax into a dedicated Social Security tax just like the tax on employers' payrolls.
>
> Such a tax would be an appropriate way to partially offset the deficit of contributions that was unavoidably created in Social

Security's early years. At that time the sensible decision was made to pay higher benefits to workers nearing retirement age than would have been possible had their benefits depended entirely on the relatively small contributions that they and their employers would have had time to make.

...

I believe we will have to earmark the estate tax in order to save it. And we should....[A] modest tax on large estates...to help pay off part of the cost of establishing a universal system of basic economic security, would be a highly progressive way to partially offset the original deficit of contributions.

Moreover, to allow the transfer of huge estates from one generation to another without paying a tax to the common good is undemocratic in principle (as Tom Paine, among other early advocates of an inheritance tax, recognized). And an analysis by the Congressional Budget Office found that a $3.5-million exemption [the exemption in 2009; it is now $5.43 million] would protect against the risk of having to break up small family farms or businesses in order to pay the tax.[17]

President Bush is no longer president, but Republicans in the House of Representatives, on April 16, 2015, passed legislation abolishing the estate tax.[18] By that vote, they made clear that they favor repeal over deficit reduction. With their vote, they have declared that the revenue is not needed to operate the government.

If that is the will of the majority in Congress and becomes law, I believe, like Bob Ball and Thomas Paine, before him, that revenues from a federal estate tax could be well used for Social Security. As Bob Ball explained, Social Security's startup costs, which benefited society as a whole, should at long last be paid back from a progressive tax. Earmarking for Social Security the revenue from the estate tax would provide a progressive way of paying down a portion of the costs appropriately incurred at the inception of the program. The eminent economists Peter Diamond and Peter Orszag named those initial costs a legacy debt. Dedicating the estate tax to pay

---

[17] Ball, "The Social Security Protection Plan," (2006), available at zfacts.com/metaPage/lib/Ball-2006-SSProtectionPlan.pdf

[18] The vote was largely along party lines, with just seven Democrats voting for repeal and just three Republicans voting against it.

those costs would appropriately be a tax on legacies to pay our nation's legacy debt.

An Expanded Social Security:
A Worldwide Beacon of Liberty, Equality, and Opportunity

More generally, the estate tax is a progressive way to restore Social Security to long range actuarial balance and expand its benefits. Expanding Social Security while requiring the wealthiest among us to pay their fair share through a dedicated Social Security estate tax is a solution to a number of challenges facing the nation.

An expanded Social Security would ameliorate the looming retirement income crisis, where too many workers fear they will never have the financial wherewithal to retire. Requiring the wealthiest estates to pay a reasonable tax would begin to slow and reverse the rapid rise in income and wealth inequality—the result, after all, of government policies redistributing income and wealth upward.

At our very founding, Thomas Paine understood the dangers of extreme income and wealth inequality not only to the general welfare of the vast majority of Americans, but to the stability of society itself. He recognized, "The plan here proposed will benefit all, without injuring any." He further recognized that his proposed estate tax, by its very justice, would "give to the accumulation of riches a degree of security" that government could not. This last point, he understood acutely, living, as he did, during the so-called Age of Revolution.

Most importantly, Paine understood that an expanded Social Security system, to which the wealthiest among us pay their fair share, will make the United States shine brighter as a beacon of freedom to the rest of the world:

> Already the conviction that government by representation is the true system of government is spreading itself fast in the world. The reasonableness of it can be seen by all. The justness of it makes itself felt even by its opposers. But when a system of civilization, (growing out of that system of government) shall be so organized that not a man or woman born in the Republic but shall inherit some means of beginning the world, and see before them the certainty of escaping the miseries that under other governments accompany old age, the [spirit of government by representation]

will have an advocate and an ally in the heart of all nations.

An army of principles will penetrate where an army of soldiers cannot; it will succeed where diplomatic management would fail: [not even]...the ocean...can arrest its progress: it will march on the horizon of the world, and it will conquer.

That "army of principles" is as powerful today as it was at the founding of the United States. Embodied in those principles are the very values that are embodied in our Social Security system. We are one United States, with one Social Security system where we share risks and responsibilities. We value freedom and justice, including the justice of the wealthiest paying their fair share. We believe in reward for hard work, as well as in the dignity and equality of each of us. Expanding Social Security, and paying the costs partly through the estate tax or another progressive tax, will reinforce those values and strengthen Thomas Paine's army of principles. Doing so will, as Paine observed at the nation's founding, generate for the United States "an advocate and an ally in the heart of all nations."

INSCRIPTION TO THE FRENCH EDITION BY THOMAS PAINE

To the Legislature and the Executive Directory of the French Republic

The plan contained in this work is not adapted for any particular country alone: the principle on which it is based is general. But as the rights of man are a new study in this world, and one needing protection from priestly imposture, and the insolence of oppressions too long established, I have thought it right to place this little work under your safeguard.

When we reflect on the long and dense night in which France and all Europe have remained plunged by their governments and their priests, we must feel less surprise than grief at the bewilderment caused by the first burst of light that dispels the darkness. The eye accustomed to darkness can hardly bear at first the broad daylight. It is by usage the eye learns to see, and it is the same in passing from any situation to its opposite.

As we have not at one instant renounced all our errors, we cannot at one stroke acquire knowledge of all our rights. France has had the honor of adding to the word *Liberty* that of *Equality*; and this word signifies essentially a principle that admits of no gradation in the things to which it applies. But equality is often misunderstood, often misapplied, and often violated.

Liberty and *Property* are words expressing all those of our possessions which are not of an intellectual nature. There are two kinds of property. Firstly, natural property, or that which comes to us from the Creator of the universe—such as the earth, air, water. Secondly, artificial or acquired property—the invention of men.

In the latter, equality is impossible; for to distribute it equally it would be necessary that all should have contributed in the same proportion, which can never be the case; and this being the case, every individual would hold on to his own property, as his right share. Equality of natural property is the subject of this little essay. Every individual in the world is born therein with legitimate claims on a certain kind of property, or its equivalent.

The right of voting for persons charged with the execution of the laws that govern society is inherent in the word liberty, and constitutes the equality of personal rights. But even if that right (of voting) were inherent in property, which I deny, the right of suffrage would still belong to all equally, because, as I have said, all individuals have legitimate birthrights in a certain species of property.

I have always considered the present Constitution of the French Republic *the best organized system* the human mind has yet produced. But I hope my former colleagues will not be offended if I warn them of an error which has slipped into its principle. Equality of the right of suffrage is not maintained. This right is in it connected with a condition on which it ought not to depend; that is, with a proportion of a certain tax called "direct."

The dignity of suffrage is thus lowered; and, in placing it in the scale with an inferior thing, the enthusiasm that right is capable of inspiring is diminished. It is impossible to find any equivalent counterpoise for the right of suffrage, because it is alone worthy to be its own basis, and cannot thrive as a graft, or an appendage.

Since the Constitution was established we have seen two conspiracies stranded—that of Babeuf, and that of some obscure personages who decorate themselves with the despicable name of "royalists." The defect in principle of the Constitution was the origin of Babeuf's conspiracy.

He availed himself of the resentment caused by this flaw, and instead of seeking a remedy by legitimate and constitutional means, or proposing some measure useful to society, the conspirators did their best to renew disorder and confusion, and constituted themselves personally into a Directory, which is formally destructive of election and representation. They were, in fine, extravagant enough to suppose that society, occupied with its domestic affairs, would blindly yield to them a directorship usurped by violence.

The conspiracy of Babeuf was followed in a few months by that of the royalists, who foolishly flattered themselves with the notion of doing great things by feeble or foul means. They counted on all the discontented, from whatever cause, and tried to rouse, in their turn, the class of people who had been following the others. But these new chiefs acted as if they thought society had nothing more at heart than to maintain courtiers, pensioners, and all their train, under the contemptible title of royalty. My little essay will disabuse them, by showing that society is aiming at a very different end—maintaining itself.

We all know or should know, that the time during which a revolution is proceeding is not the time when its resulting advantages can be enjoyed. But had Babeuf and his accomplices taken into consideration the condition of France under this Constitution, and compared it with what it was under the tragical revolutionary government, and during the execrable Reign of Terror, the rapidity of the alteration must have appeared to them very striking and astonishing. Famine has been replaced by abundance, and by the well-founded hope of a near and increasing prosperity.

As for the defect in the Constitution, I am fully convinced that it will be rectified constitutionally, and that this step is indispensable; for so long as it continues it will inspire the hopes and furnish the means of conspirators; and for the rest, it is regrettable that a Constitution so wisely organized should err so much in its principle. This fault exposes it to other dangers which will make themselves felt.

Intriguing candidates will go about among those who have not the means to pay the direct tax and pay it for them, on condition of receiving their votes. Let us maintain inviolably equality in the sacred right of suffrage: public security can never have a basis more solid. *Salut et Fraternité*.

Your former colleague,
Thomas Paine

ENGLISH PREFACE BY THOMAS PAINE

The following little piece was written in the winter of 1795 and '96; and, as I had not determined whether to publish it during the present war, or to wait till the commencement of a peace, it has lain by me, without alteration or addition, from the time it was written.

What has determined me to publish it now is a sermon preached by Watson, Bishop of Llandaff. Some of my readers will recollect, that this Bishop wrote a book entitled "An Apology for the Bible," in answer to my second part of "The Age of Reason." I procured a copy of his book, and he may depend upon hearing from me on that subject.

At the end of the Bishop's book is a list of the works he has written. Among which is the sermon alluded to; it is entitled: "The Wisdom and Goodness of God, in having made both Rich and Poor; with an Appendix, containing Reflections on the Present State of England and France."

The error contained in this sermon determined me to publish my "Agrarian Justice." It is wrong to say God made *rich* and *poor;* He made only *male* and *female,* and He gave them the earth for their inheritance.

Instead of preaching to encourage one part of mankind in insolence . . . it would be better that priests employed their time to render the general condition of man less miserable than it is. Practical religion consists in doing good: and the only way of serving God is that of endeavoring to make His creation happy. All preaching that has not this for its object is nonsense and hypocrisy.

Thomas Paine

AGRARIAN JUSTICE

To preserve the benefits of what is called civilized life, and to remedy at the same time the evil which it has produced, ought to considered as one of the first objects of reformed legislation.

Whether that state that is proudly, perhaps erroneously, called civilization, has most promoted or most injured the general happiness of man is a question that may be strongly contested. On one side, the spectator is dazzled by splendid appearances; on the other, he is shocked by extremes of wretchedness; both of which it has erected. The most affluent and the most miserable of the human race are to be found in the countries that are called civilized.

To understand what the state of society ought to be, it is necessary to have some idea of the natural and primitive state of man; such as it is at this day among the Indians of North America. There is not, in that state, any of those spectacles of human misery which poverty and want present to our eyes in all the towns and streets in Europe.

Poverty, therefore, is a thing created by that which is called civilized life. It exists not in the natural state. On the other hand, the natural state is without those advantages which flow from agriculture, arts, science and manufactures.

The life of an Indian is a continual holiday, compared with the poor of Europe; and, on the other hand it appears to be abject when compared to the rich. Civilization, therefore, or that which is so-called, has operated two ways: to make one part of society more affluent, and the other more wretched, than would have been the lot of either in a natural state.

It is always possible to go from the natural to the civilized state, but it is never possible to go from the civilized to the natural state. The reason is that man in a natural state, subsisting by hunting, requires ten times the quantity of land to range over to procure himself sustenance, than would support him in a civilized state, where the earth is cultivated.

When, therefore, a country becomes populous by the additional aids of cultivation, art and science, there is a necessity of preserving things in that state; because without it there cannot be sustenance for more, perhaps, than a tenth part of its inhabitants. The thing, therefore, now to be done is to remedy the evils and preserve the benefits that have arisen to society by passing from the natural to that which is called the civilized state.

In taking the matter upon this ground, the first principle of civilization ought to have been, and ought still to be, that the condition of every person born into the world, after a state of civilization commences, ought not to be worse than if he had been born before that period.

But the fact is that the condition of millions, in every country in Europe, is far worse than if they had been born before civilization began, had been born among the Indians of North America at the present. I will show how this fact has happened.

It is a position not to be controverted that the earth, in its natural, cultivated state was, and ever would have continued to be, *the common property of the human race*. In that state every man would have been born to property. He would have been a joint life proprietor with rest in the property of the soil, and in all its natural productions, vegetable and animal.

But the earth in its natural state, as before said, is capable of supporting but a small number of inhabitants compared with what it is capable of doing in a cultivated state. And as it is impossible to separate the improvement made by cultivation from the earth itself, upon which that improvement is made, the idea of landed property arose from that parable connection; but it is nevertheless true, that it is the value of the improvement, only, and not the earth itself, that is individual property.

Every proprietor, therefore, of cultivated lands, owes to the community a *ground-rent* (for I know of no better term to express the idea) for the land which he holds; and it is from this ground-rent that the fund proposed in this plan is to issue.

It is deducible, as well from the nature of the thing as from all the stories transmitted to us, that the idea of landed property commenced with cultivation, and that there was no such thing as landed property before that time. It could not exist in the first state of man, that of hunters. It did not exist in the second state, that of shepherds: neither Abraham, Isaac, Jacob, nor Job, so far as the history of the Bible may credited in probable things, were owners of land.

Their property consisted, as is always enumerated in flocks and herds, they traveled with them from place to place. The frequent contentions at that time about the use of a well in the dry country of Arabia, where those people lived, also show that there was no landed property. It was not admitted that land could be claimed as property.

There could be no such thing as landed property originally. Man did not make the earth, and, though he had a natural right to *occupy* it, he had no right to *locate as his property* in perpetuity any part of it; neither did the Creator of the earth open a land-office, from whence the first title-deeds should issue. Whence then, arose the idea of landed property? I answer as before, that when cultivation began the idea of landed property began with it, from the impossibility of separating the improvement made by cultivation from the earth itself, upon which that improvement was made.

The value of the improvement so far exceeded the value of the natural earth, at that time, as to absorb it; till, in the end, the common right of all became confounded into the cultivated right of the individual. But there are, nevertheless, distinct species of rights, and will continue to be, so long as the earth endures.

It is only by tracing things to their origin that we can gain rightful ideas of them, and it is by gaining such ideas that we discover the boundary that divides right from wrong, and teaches every man to know his own. I have entitled this tract "Agrarian Justice" to distinguish it from "Agrarian Law."

Nothing could be more unjust than agrarian law in a country improved by cultivation; for though every man, as an inhabitant of the earth, is a joint proprietor of it in its natural state, it does not follow that he is a joint proprietor of cultivated earth. The additional value made by cultivation, after the system was admitted, became the property of those who did it, or who inherited it from them, or who purchased it. It had originally no owner. While, therefore, I advocate the right, and interest myself in the hard case of all those who have been thrown out of their natural inheritance by the introduction of the system of landed property, I equally defend the right of the possessor to the part which is his.

Cultivation is at least one of the greatest natural improvements ever made by human invention. It has given to created earth a tenfold value. But the landed monopoly that began with it has produced the greatest evil. It has dispossessed more than half the inhabitants of every nation of their natural inheritance, without providing for them, as ought to have been done, an indemnification for that loss, and has thereby created a species of poverty and wretchedness that did not exist before.

In advocating the case of the persons thus dispossessed, it is a right, and not a charity, that I am pleading for. But it is that kind of right which, being neglected at first, could not be brought forward afterwards till heaven had opened the way by a revolution in the system of government. Let us then do honor to revolutions by justice, and give currency to their principles by blessings.

Having thus in a few words, opened the merits of the case, I shall now proceed to the plan I have to propose, which is,

To create a national fund, out of which there shall be paid to every person, when arrived at the age of twenty-one years, the sum of fifteen pounds sterling, as a compensation in part, for the loss of his or her natural inheritance, by the introduction of the system of landed property:

And also, the sum of ten pounds per annum, during life, to every person now living, of the age of fifty years, and to all others as they shall arrive at that age.

Means by Which the Fund Is to Be Created

I have already established the principle, namely, that the earth, in its natural uncultivated state was, and ever would have continued to be, the *common property of the human race;* that in that state, every person would have been born to property; and that the system of landed property, by its inseparable connection with cultivation, and with what is called civilized life, has absorbed the property of all those whom it dispossessed, without providing, as ought to have been done, an indemnification for that loss.

The fault, however, is not in the present possessors. No complaint is tended, or ought to be alleged against them, unless they adopt the crime by opposing justice. The fault is in the system, and it has stolen perceptibly upon the world, aided afterwards by the agrarian law of the sword. But the fault can be made to reform itself by successive generations; and without diminishing or deranging the property of any of present possessors, the operation of the fund can yet commence, and in full activity, the first year of its establishment, or soon after, as I shall show.

It is proposed that the payments, as already stated, be made to every person, rich or poor. It is best to make it so, to prevent invidious distinctions. It is also right it should be so, because it is in lieu of the natural inheritance, which, as a right, belongs to every man, over and above property he may have created, or inherited from those who did. Such persons as do not choose to receive it can throw it into the common fund.

Taking it then for granted that no person ought to be in a worse condition when born under what is called a state of civilization, than he would have been had he been born in a state of nature, and that civilization ought to have made, and ought still to make, provision for that purpose, it can only be done by subtracting from property a portion equal in value to the natural inheritance it has absorbed.

Various methods may be proposed for this purpose, but that which appears to be the best (not only because it will operate without deranging any present possessors, or without interfering with the collection of taxes or *emprunts* necessary for the purposes of government and the Revolution, but because it will be the least troublesome and the most effectual, and also because the subtraction will be made at a time that best admits it) is at the moment that property is passing by the death of one person to the possession of another. In this case, the bequeather gives nothing: the receiver pays nothing. The only matter to him is that the monopoly of natural inheritance, to which there never was a right, begins to cease in his person. A generous man would not wish it to continue, and a just man will rejoice to see it abolished.

My state of health prevents my making sufficient inquiries with respect to the doctrine of probabilities, whereon to found calculations with such degrees of certainty as they are capable of. What, therefore, I offer on this head is more the result of observation and reflection than of received information; but I believe it will be found to agree sufficiently with fact. In the first place, taking twenty-one years as the epoch of maturity, all the property of a nation, real and personal, is always in the possession of persons above that age. It is then necessary to know, as a datum of calculation, the average of years which persons above that age will live. I take this average to be about thirty years, for though many persons will live forty, fifty, or sixty years, after the age of twenty-one years, others will die much sooner, and some in every year of that time.

Taking, then, thirty years as the average of time, it will give, without any material variation one way or other, the average of time in which the whole property or capital of a nation, or a sum equal thereto, will have passed through one entire revolution in descent, that is, will have gone by deaths to new possessors; for though, in many instances, some parts of this capital will remain forty, fifty, or sixty years in the possession of one person, other parts will have revolved two or three times before those thirty years expire, which will bring it to that average; for were one-half the capital of a nation to revolve twice in thirty years, it would produce the same fund as if the whole revolved once.

Taking, then, thirty years as the average of time in which the whole capital of a nation, or a sum equal thereto, will revolve once, the thirtieth part thereof will be the sum that will revolve every year, that is, will go by deaths to new possessors; and this last sum being thus known, and the ratio per cent to be subtracted from it determined, it will give the annual amount or income of the proposed fund, to be applied as already mentioned.

In looking over the discourse of the English Minister, Pitt, in his opening of what is called in England the budget (the scheme of finance for the year 1796), I find an estimate of the national capital of that unity. As this estimate of a national capital is prepared ready to my hand, I take it as a datum to act upon. When a calculation is made upon the known capital of any nation, combined with its population, it will serve as a scale for any other nation, in proportion as its capital and population be more or less.

I am the more disposed to take this estimate of Mr. Pitt, for the purpose of showing to that minister, upon his own calculation, how much better money may be employed than in wasting it, as he has done, on the wild project of setting up Bourbon kings. What, in the name of heaven, are Bourbon kings to the people of England? It is better that the people have bread.

Mr. Pitt states the national capital of England, real and personal, to one thousand three hundred millions sterling, which is about one-fourth part of the national capital of France, including Belgia. The event of the last harvest in each country proves that the soil of France more productive than that of England, and that it can better support twenty-four or twenty-five millions of inhabitants than that of England can seven or seven and a half millions.

The thirtieth part of this capital of £1,300,000,000 is £43,333,333 which is the part that will revolve every year by deaths in that country to new possessors; and the sum that will annually revolve in France in the proportion of four to one, will be about one hundred and seventy-three millions sterling. From this sum of £43,333,333 annually revolving, is to be subtracted the value of the natural inheritance absorbed in it, which, perhaps, in fair justice, cannot be taken at less, and ought not be taken for more, than a tenth part.

It will always happen that of the property thus revolving by deaths every year a part will descend in a direct line to sons and daughters, and the other part collaterally, and the proportion will be found to be about three to one; that is, about thirty millions of the above sum will descend to direct heirs, and the remaining sum of £413,333,333 to more distant relations, and in part to strangers.

Considering, then, that man is always related to society, that relationship will become comparatively greater in proportion as the next of kin is more distant; it is therefore consistent with civilization to say that where there are no direct heirs society shall be heir to a part over and above the tenth part *due* to society.

If this additional part be from five to ten or twelve per cent, in proportion as the next of kin be nearer or more remote, so as to average with the escheats that may fall, which ought always to go to society and not to the government (an addition of ten per cent more), the produce from the annual sum of £43,333,333 will be:

From £30,000,000	at ten per cent	£3,000,000
From £13,333,333	at ten per cent with the addition of ten per cent more	£2,666,666
£43,333,333		£5,666,666

Having thus arrived at the annual amount of the proposed fund, I come, in the next place, to speak of the population proportioned to this fund and to compare it with the uses to which the fund is to be applied.

The population (I mean that of England) does not exceed seven millions and a half, and the number of persons above the age of fifty will in that case be about four hundred thousand. There would not, however, be more than that number that would accept the proposed ten pounds sterling per annum, though they would be entitled to it. I have no idea it would be accepted by many persons who had a yearly income of two or three hundred pounds sterling. But as we often see instances of rich people falling into sudden poverty, even at the age of sixty, they would always have the right of drawing all the arrears due to them. Four millions, therefore, of the above annual sum of £5,666,666 will be required for four hundred thousand aged persons, at ten pounds sterling each.

I come now to speak of the persons annually arriving at twenty-one years of age. If all the persons who died were above the age of twenty-one years, the number of persons annually arriving at that age must be equal to the annual number of deaths, to keep the population stationary. But the greater part die under the age of twenty-one, and therefore the number of persons annually arriving at twenty-one will be less than half the number of deaths.

The whole number of deaths upon a population of seven millions and a half will be about 220,000 annually. The number arriving at twenty-one years of age will be about 100,000. The whole number of these will not receive the proposed fifteen pounds, for the reasons already mentioned, though, as in the former case, they would be entitled to it. Admitting then that a tenth part declined receiving it, the amount would stand thus:

Fund annually		£5,666,666
To 400,000 aged persons at £10 each	£4,000,000	
To 90,000 persons of 21 yrs., £15 ster. each	£1,350,000	
		£5,350,000
Remains		£316,666

There are, in every country, a number of blind and lame persons totally incapable of earning a livelihood. But as it will always happen that the greater number of blind persons will be among those who are above the age of fifty years, they will be provided for in that class. The remaining sum of £316,666 will provide for the lame and blind under that age, at the same rate of £10 annually for each person.

Having now gone through all the necessary calculations, and stated the particulars of the plan, I shall conclude with some observations.

It is not charity but a right, not bounty but justice, that I am pleading for. The present state of civilization is as odious as it is unjust. It is absolutely the opposite of what it should be, and it is necessary that a revolution should be made in it. The contrast of affluence and wretchedness continually meeting and offending the eye, is like dead and living bodies chained together. Though I care as little about riches as any man, I am a friend to riches because they are capable of good.

I care not how affluent some may be, provided that none be miserable in consequence of it. But it is impossible to enjoy affluence with the felicity it is capable of being enjoyed, while so much misery is mingled in the scene. The sight of the misery, and the unpleasant sensations it suggests, which, though they may be suffocated cannot be extinguished, are a greater drawback upon the felicity of affluence than the proposed ten per cent upon property is worth. He that would not give the one to get rid of the other has no charity, even for himself.

There are, in every country, some magnificent charities established by individuals. It is, however, but little that any individual can do, when the whole extent of the misery to be relieved is considered. He may satisfy his conscience, but not his heart. He may give all that he has, and that all will relieve but little. It is only by organizing civilization upon such principles as to act like a system of pulleys, that the whole weight of misery can be removed.

The plan here proposed will reach the whole. It will immediately relieve and take out of view three classes of wretchedness—the blind, the lame, and the aged poor; and it will furnish the rising generation with means to prevent their becoming poor; and it will do this without deranging or interfering with any national measures.

To show that this will be the case, it is sufficient to observe that the operation and effect of the plan will, in all cases, be the same as if every individual were *voluntarily* to make his will and dispose of his property in the manner here proposed.

But it is justice, and not charity, that is the principle of the plan. In all great cases it is necessary to have a principle more universally active than charity; and, with respect to justice, it ought not to be left to the choice of detached individuals whether they will do justice or not. Considering, then, the plan on the ground of justice, it ought to be the act of the whole growing spontaneously out of the principles of the revolution, and the reputation of it ought to be national and not individual.

A plan upon this principle would benefit the revolution by the energy that springs from the consciousness of justice. It would multiply also the national resources; for property, like vegetation, increases by offsets. When a young couple begin the world, the difference is exceedingly great whether they begin with nothing or with fifteen pounds apiece. With this aid they could buy a cow, and implements to cultivate a few acres of land; and instead of becoming burdens upon society, which is always the case where children are produced faster than they can be fed, would be put in the way of becoming useful and profitable citizens. The national domains also would sell the better if pecuniary aids were provided to cultivate them in small lots.

It is the practice of what has unjustly obtained the name of civilization (and the practice merits not to be called either charity or policy) to make some provision for persons becoming poor and wretched only at the time they become so. Would it not, even as a matter of economy, be far better to adopt means to prevent their becoming poor? This can best be done by making every person when arrived at the age of twenty-one years an inheritor of something to begin with.

The rugged face of society, checkered with the extremes of affluence and want, proves that some extraordinary violence has been committed upon it, and calls on justice for redress. The great mass of the poor in countries are become an hereditary race, and it is next to impossible them to get out of that state of themselves. It ought also to be observed that this mass increases in all countries that are called civilized. More persons fall annually into it than get out of it.

Though in a plan of which justice and humanity are the foundation principles, interest ought not to be admitted into the calculation, yet it is always of advantage to the establishment of any plan to show that it beneficial as a matter of interest. The success of any proposed plan submitted to public consideration must finally depend on the numbers interested in supporting it, united with the justice of its principles.

The plan here proposed will benefit all, without injuring any. It will consolidate the interest of the republic with that of the individual. To the numerous class dispossessed of their natural inheritance by the system of landed property it will be an act of national justice. To persons dying possessed of moderate fortunes it will operate as a tontine to their children, more beneficial than the sum of money paid into the fund: and it will give to the accumulation of riches a degree of security that none of old governments of Europe, now tottering on their foundations, can give.

I do not suppose that more than one family in ten, in any of the countries of Europe, has, when the head of the family dies, a clear property of five hundred pounds sterling. To all such the plan is advantageous. That property would pay fifty pounds into the fund, and if there were only two children under age they would receive fifteen pounds each (thirty pounds), on coming of age, and be entitled to ten pounds a year after fifty.

It is from the overgrown acquisition of property that the fund will support itself; and I know that the possessors of such property in England, though they would eventually be benefitted by the protection of nine-tenths of it, will exclaim against the plan. But without entering any inquiry how they came by that property, let them recollect that they have been the advocates of this war, and that Mr. Pitt has already laid on more new taxes to be raised annually upon the people of England, and that for supporting the despotism of Austria and the Bourbons against the liberties of France, than would pay annually all the sums proposed in this plan.

I have made the calculations stated in this plan, upon what is called personal, as well as upon landed property. The reason for making it upon land is already explained; and the reason for taking personal property into the calculation is equally well founded though on a different principle. Land, as before said, is the free gift of the Creator in common to the human race. Personal property is the *effect of society;* and it is as impossible for an individual to acquire personal property without the aid of society, as it is for him to make land originally.

Separate an individual from society, and give him an island or a continent to possess, and he cannot acquire personal property. He cannot be rich. So inseparably are the means connected with the end, in all cases, that where the former do not exist the latter cannot be obtained. All accumulation, therefore, of personal property, beyond what a man's own hands produce, is derived to him by living in society; and he owes on every principle of justice, of gratitude, and of civilization, a part of that accumulation back again to society from whence the whole came.

This is putting the matter on a general principle, and perhaps it is best to do so; for if we examine the case minutely it will be found that the accumulation of personal property is, in many instances, the effect of paying too little for the labor that produced it; the consequence of which is that the working hand perishes in old age, and the employer abounds in affluence.

It is, perhaps, impossible to proportion exactly the price of labor to the profits it produces; and it will also be said, as an apology for the injustice, that were a workman to receive an increase of wages daily he would not save it against old age, nor be much better for it in the interim. Make, then, society the treasurer to guard it for him in a common fund; for it is no reason that, because he might not make a good use of it for himself, another should take it.

The state of civilization that has prevailed throughout Europe, is as unjust in its principle, as it is horrid in its effects; and it is the consciousness of this, and the apprehension that such a state cannot continue when once investigation begins in any country, that makes the possessors of property dread every idea of a revolution. It is the hazard and not the principle of revolutions that retards their progress. This being the case, it is necessary as well for the protection of property as for the sake of justice and humanity, to form a system that, while it preserves one part of society from wretchedness, shall secure the other from depreciation.

The superstitious awe, the enslaving reverence, that formerly surrounded affluence, is passing away in all countries, and leaving the possessor of property to the convulsion of accidents. When wealth and splendor, instead of fascinating the multitude, excite emotions of disgust; when, instead of drawing forth admiration, it is beheld as an insult on wretchedness; when the ostentatious appearance it makes serves call the right of it in question, the case of property becomes critical, and it is only in a system of justice that the possessor can contemplate security.

To remove the danger, it is necessary to remove the antipathies, and this can only be done by making property productive of a national blessing, extending to every individual. When the riches of one man above other shall increase the national fund in the same proportion; when it shall be seen that the prosperity of that fund depends on the prosperity of individuals; when the more riches a man acquires, the better it shall be for the general mass; it is then that antipathies will cease, and property be placed on the permanent basis of national interest and protection.

I have no property in France to become subject to the plan I propose. What I have, which is not much, is in the United States of America. But I will pay one hundred pounds sterling toward this fund in France, the instant it shall be established; and I will pay the same sum England, whenever a similar establishment shall take place in that country.

A revolution in the state of civilization is the necessary companion of revolutions in the system of government. If a revolution in any country be from bad to good, or from good to bad, the state of what is called civilization in that country, must be made conformable thereto, to give that revolution effect.

Despotic government supports itself by abject civilization, in which debasement of the human mind, and wretchedness in the mass of the people, are the chief criterions. Such governments consider man merely as an animal; that the exercise of intellectual faculty is not his privilege; *that he has nothing to do with the laws but to obey them;* and they politically depend more upon breaking the spirit of the people by poverty, than they fear enraging it by desperation.

It is a revolution in the state of civilization that will give perfection to Revolution of France. Already the conviction that government by representation is the true system of government is spreading itself fast in the world. The reasonableness of it can be seen by all. The justness of it makes itself felt even by its opposers. But when a system of civilization, (growing out of that system of government) shall be so organized that not a man or woman born in the Republic but shall inherit some means of beginning the world, and see before them the certainty of escaping the miseries that under other governments accompany old age, the Revolution of France will have an advocate and an ally in the heart of all nations.

An army of principles will penetrate where an army of soldiers cannot; it will succeed where diplomatic management would fail: it is neither the Rhine, the Channel, nor the ocean that can arrest its progress: it will march on the horizon of the world, and it will conquer.

Means for Carrying the Proposed Plan into Execution, and to Render it at the Same Time Conducive to the Public Interest

I. Each canton shall elect in its primary assemblies, three persons, as commissioners for that canton, who shall take cognizance, and keep a register of all matters happening in that canton, conformable to the charter that shall be established by law for carrying this plan into execution.

II. The law shall fix the manner in which the property of deceased persons shall be ascertained.

III. When the amount of the property of any deceased persons shall be ascertained, the principal heir to that property, or the eldest of the co-heirs, if of lawful age, or if under age, the person authorized by the will of the deceased to represent him or them, shall give bond to the commissioners of the canton to pay the said tenth part thereof in four equal quarterly payments, within the space of one year or sooner, at the choice of the payers. One-half of the whole property shall remain as a security until the bond be paid off.

IV. The bond shall be registered in the office of the commissioners of the canton, and the original bonds shall be deposited in the national bank at Paris. The bank shall publish every quarter of a year the amount of the bonds in its possession, and also the bonds that shall have been paid off, or what parts thereof, since the last quarterly publication.

The national bank shall issue bank notes upon the security of the bonds in its possession. The notes so issued, shall be applied to pay the pensions of aged persons, and the compensations to persons arriving at twenty-one years of age. It is both reasonable and generous to suppose, that persons not under immediate necessity, will suspend their right of drawing on the fund, until it acquire, as it will do, a greater degree of ability. In this case, it is proposed, that an honorary register be kept, in each canton, of the names of the persons thus suspending that right, at least during the present war.

VI. As the inheritors of property must always take up their bonds in four quarterly payments, or sooner if they choose, there will always be *numeraire* arriving at the bank after the expiration of the first quarter, to exchange for the bank notes that shall be brought in.

VII. The bank notes being thus put in circulation, upon the best of all possible security, that of actual property, to more than four times the amount of the bonds upon which the notes are issued, and with *numeraire* continually arriving at the bank to exchange or pay them off whenever they shall be presented for that purpose, they will acquire a permanent value in all parts of the Republic. They can therefore be received in payment of taxes, or emprunts equal to *numeraire*, because the Government can always receive *numeraire* for them at the bank.

VIII. It will be necessary that the payments of the ten per cent be made in *numeraire* for the first year from the establishment of the plan. But after the expiration of the first year, the inheritors of property may pay ten per cent either in bank notes issued upon the fund, or in *numeraire*.

If the payments be in *numeraire*, it will lie as a deposit at the bank, be exchanged for a quantity of notes equal to that amount; and if in notes issued upon the fund, it will cause a demand upon the fund equal thereto; and thus the operation of the plan will create means to carry itself into execution.

Thomas Paine

ABOUT THE AUTHOR

Nancy J. Altman has a forty year background in the areas of Social Security and private pensions. She is co-director of Social Security Works and co-chair of the Strengthen Social Security coalition. She is the author of *The Battle for Social Security: From FDR's Vision to Bush's Gamble* (John Wiley & Sons, 2005), and co-author of *Social Security Works! Why Social Security Isn't Going Broke and How Expanding It Will Help Us All* (The New Press, 2015).

From 1983 to 1989, Ms. Altman was on the faculty of Harvard University's Kennedy School of Government and taught courses on private pensions and Social Security at the Harvard Law School. In 1982, she was Alan Greenspan's assistant in his position as chairman of the bipartisan commission that developed the 1983 Social Security amendments. From 1977 to 1981, she was a legislative assistant to Senator John C. Danforth (R-MO), and advised the Senator with respect to Social Security issues. From 1974 to 1977, she was a tax lawyer with Covington & Burling, where she handled a variety of private pension matters.

Ms. Altman is the Chairman of the Board of Directors of the Pension Rights Center, a nonprofit organization dedicated to the protection of beneficiary rights. She is also on the Board of Directors of the National Academy of Social Insurance, a membership organization of over 900 of the nation's leading experts on social insurance. In the mid-1980's, she was on the organizing committee and the first board of directors of the National Academy of Social Insurance.

Ms. Altman has an A.B. from Harvard University and a J.D. from the University of Pennsylvania Law School.

Printed in Great Britain
by Amazon.co.uk, Ltd.,
Marston Gate.